HISTORIC PHOTOS OF
EL PASO

TEXT AND CAPTIONS BY SANDRA FYE

TURNER
PUBLISHING COMPANY

The McGinty Club picnic at Orn's Grove, in 1892. The McGinty Club was a group of men who liked to drink, play music, march, have parades, and have a good time. The club was led by Daniel W. Reckbart and was named after a song that was popular at the time. In the early days of El Paso, the McGinty Club provided the community with comedy and other entertainment and always made a point to dress well. The club was active until about 1905, when members formed other clubs, such as the Toltec Club.

HISTORIC PHOTOS OF
EL PASO

Turner Publishing Company
www.turnerpublishing.com

Historic Photos of El Paso

Copyright © 2008 Turner Publishing Company

Library of Congress Control Number: 2007941395

ISBN: 978-1-59652-430-9

Printed in the United States

ISBN 978-1-68442-006-3 (hc)

Contents

The Rio Grande Valley Bank and Trust Building, which later became the Abdou Building, at 115 North Mesa Street in 1910. The exposed concrete structure was then the tallest building in El Paso. The bank was on the first two floors, while the upper floors housed the professional offices of the law firms of Bates McFarland; R. C. Walsh; C. W. Marshall; Goodwell and Sweeney; and the dental practice of Brandy and Letord.

ACKNOWLEDGMENTS

With the exception of cropping images where needed and touching up imperfections that have accrued over time, no other changes have been made to the photographs in this volume. The caliber and clarity of many photographs are limited by the technology of the day and the ability of the photographer at the time they were made.

This volume, *Historic Photos of El Paso,* is the result of the cooperation and efforts of many individuals, organizations, and corporations. It is with great thanks that we acknowledge the valuable contribution of the following for their generous support:

El Paso County Historical Society
El Paso Public Library
Library of Congress

The El Paso Public Library provided a nice environment to learn about the history of El Paso. Danny Gonzalez and Claudia Ramirez had photographs from the Border Heritage Center set aside for me to look at, which was a very big help. I am grateful for the information available on the World Wide Web and thank all of you who post historical articles. For the loan of El Paso books and the enthusiastic sharing of El Paso stories, thank you Stefan Kosicki. To Lieutenant Colonel Rufino De La Cruz, USMC retired; Vanessa De La Cruz; and Juliette De La Cruz, I appreciate the help identifying pictures. Glenn, Mo, and Debbi provided help and encouragement; muchas gracias a mis amigos. I hope you all enjoy the book!

—*Sandra Fye*

PREFACE

Native Americans have been in the El Paso area for around 10,000 years. The Keystone Wetlands and Hueco Tanks sites are both about 4,500 years old. The native people followed the Rio Grande and traded along its path. In 1598, Don Juan de Oñate traveled north along the Rio Grande with a large caravan from Zacatecas, Mexico, to what became known as El Paso del Norte. Near San Elizario, Oñate claimed the area for Spain, and it became a trade center along El Camino Real, the Royal Highway, which went north all the way to the Española Valley in New Mexico.

In 1659, a mission was founded at what is now Ciudad Juárez to convert the Manso people to Catholicism. Mission Nuestra Señora de Guadalupe was started in 1662, and when finished in 1668 was considered the best in the Custodia de Nuevo México. During the Pueblo Revolt of 1680, about 2,000 people traveled south to El Paso del Norte missions to seek refuge.

Mexico won its independence from Spain in 1821, so the area became part of Mexico, and trade was allowed with the United States. This part of the Camino Real became known as the Chihuahuan Trail. In 1845, the Republic of Texas became part of the United States, and the settlement of Franklin was started on the north side of the Rio Grande. With the 1848 signing of the Treaty of Guadalupe Hidalgo, the Rio Grande became the international boundary between the United States and Mexico.

In 1848, the United States Army sent units to defend the territory gained in the Mexican War, protect settlers, and maintain the law. Two infantry companies were stationed at San Elizario and four at the Post Opposite El Paso, later re-named Fort Bliss, across the Rio Grande from the settlement then called El Paso del Norte. In 1890, legislation was passed to construct new Fort Bliss buildings at La Noria Mesa, near Concordia. The construction was completed in 1893.

In 1852, a post office was established at Franklin. The Butterfield Overland Mail and Stage arrived in 1858 and passed through twice a week. Brigadier General Anson Mills built the station and corrals for the stage on two acres at El Paso,

Overland, and Oregon streets. Across the street from the station was the post office, a store, and a bar. In 1859, Mills surveyed the town, and the sketch of it shows a plaza, a public square, streets, and the *acequia madre* (mother irrigation ditch) east of the plaza. Mills also changed the name of Franklin to El Paso. Magoffinsville, Hart's Mill, and Concordia were settlements in the area. El Paso was incorporated as a city in 1873. Across the river, El Paso del Norte was renamed Ciudad Juárez in 1888.

The arrival of the Southern Pacific; the Texas and Pacific; and the Atchison, Topeka and Santa Fe railroads in 1881 brought in many people, including the Chinese laborers who built them. El Paso was considered a Wild West outpost and had gunfighters, prostitutes, gamblers, outlaws, and dancehall girls. The El Paso and Southwestern Railroad, owned by the Phelps-Dodge Company, brought copper to El Paso from Bisbee, Arizona.

El Paso had roughly 4,000 residents in 1909 when photographer Otis Aultman moved there. He was 35 years old and had learned photography from his brother. Hired by Homer A. Scott, of the Scott Photo Company, Aultman took pictures of the historic 1909 meeting between presidents William Howard Taft of the United States and Porfirio Díaz of Mexico. Over time, news photos by Aultman would be featured often in full-page spreads in the El Paso papers. He also did commercial photography for the architecture firm of Trost and Trost, and with an interest in archaeology and history, he served as vice-president of the El Paso Archaeological Society.

On March 5, 1943, Aultman died in his studio. His photograph collection, from which many of the historic images in this book have been drawn, now resides at the El Paso Public Library.

—Sandra Fye

A tranquil walk down Montana Avenue. The 1000–1500 section of Montana Avenue is a historic district on the National Register of Historic Places. Henry C. Trost built many of the homes there, which now house offices and apartments.

The Early Days of El Paso

(1880–1899)

The building of the railroad changed El Paso from a village into a town. Before the Southern Pacific line arrived, on May 26, 1881, the region's population was in the neighborhood of a mere few thousand. The inhabitants and their businesses included merchants, traders along the Chihuahua Trail, freight companies, soldiers, miners, ranchers, farms, hotels, bars, dry goods stores, butchers, military contractors selling supplies, missionaries, and outlaws.

Some of the Chinese laborers who built the railroads stayed in El Paso to operate boardinghouses, laundries, stores, farms, and restaurants. Gambling halls, saloons, and prostitution houses were plentiful in the early days. A custom smelter built by Robert Towne in 1887 brought many other businesses. Mines in Chihuahua, Arizona, New Mexico, and Texas used the railroad to bring in minerals, which in turn brought investors to Mexico and El Paso.

El Paso del Norte became Ciudad Juárez in 1888. It was named to honor Benito Juárez, and Ciudad Juárez had a huge celebration with games and entertainment. The city attracted many visitors and businessmen who enjoyed such varied facets as the Guadalupe Mission and the local stores, music, cockfights, and gambling establishments. The more affluent residents owned elaborate haciendas with vineyards and gardens.

Ranching, mining, smelting, the military, and the railroad brought many new residents to El Paso, often with families. Churches, clubs, and schools were organized. People from Mexico moved north for jobs and commerce. A fountain in El Paso's central plaza had alligators living in it that residents and visitors always loved to watch.

Company A of the Twenty-fifth Infantry, a regiment of African American soldiers, came to Fort Bliss in 1899. The soldiers built forts, roads, guarded the border, escorted the U.S. mail, and enforced treaties. The Native Americans called them Buffalo Soldiers, and they had a reputation for being high-quality professionals. Twenty-eight Buffalo Soldiers are buried in the Concordia Cemetery.

The *Lone Star* Building stood at 10 West Overland Avenue. The *Lone Star* was a newspaper owned by Simeon Harrison Newman that appeared on Wednesdays and Saturdays starting in 1881. Newman was involved in city politics and the founding of the White Oaks Railroad. He fought for public schools, good utilities, and a fire department, using his newspaper as a forum for his ideas.

Seeing the Santa Fe Deluxe pulling into the Santa Fe Depot, at Fifth and Santa Fe streets, created a lot of excitement for the people of El Paso. The sleepy little town of about a thousand residents in 1881 can be seen behind the station and the Santa Fe Deluxe Number 36. The Southern Pacific Railroad beat the Santa Fe into El Paso, however, with the May 26, 1881, arrival of the first train into town.

Looking northeast, from San Jacinto Plaza, toward the Franklin Mountains. The Gilbert brothers donated the land for a town square in 1857. The plaza was a pleasant place to stroll with friends and family and to enjoy the view of the mountains, especially at sunrise and sunset. Many people still enjoy walking around San Jacinto Plaza and sitting on the plaza benches talking to friends.

This is a typical adobe home of the late nineteenth century. Hornos (adobe ovens) were used to bake bread, corn, and tortillas. Adobe bricks are made of mud and straw, then sun-dried in forms, typically with the whole family helping in the enterprise. In 1854, when the area was known as Franklin, adobe homes were along the trail that was to become El Paso Street. When the railroads were built to El Paso, many other types of building materials started being used.

The mule car trolley is passing the O. T. Bassett Lumber Company, at North Mill and Stanton Street. Oscar T. Bassett met Charles Morehead while the two were traveling by stage to El Paso in 1880. When they arrived in El Paso, they had dinner with Mayor Joseph Magoffin and bought 400 acres of land from him for the Texas and Pacific Railroad. Bassett, Morehead, and a group of St. Louis investors started the State National Bank in 1881.

Fort Bliss at Hart's Mill, where Mexican War veteran Simeon Hart had his flour mill, El Molino. After the regional "Salt War" violence of 1877, the United States government bought 135 acres at Hart's Mill for Fort Bliss. In 1893, Fort Bliss moved to La Noria Mesa. The fort was named after Mexican War veteran Lieutenant Colonel William Wallace Smith Bliss.

The Treaty of Guadalupe Hidalgo, in 1848, ended the Mexican War, and the United States acquired a vast area north of the Rio Grande. A treaty signed on May 21, 1906, guaranteed Mexico 60,000 acre feet of water from the Rio Grande.

South El Paso Street was the center of town, as seen here in 1882. The sign on the right is for the Pony Saloon, which has a stack of empty beer barrels next to it. El Paso Street was the scene of a famous shootout involving Marshal Dallas Stoudenmire, John Hale, Gus Krempkau, and George Campbell. Stoudenmire was killed in a saloon on El Paso Street in September 1882. Masonic Lodge No. 130 paid for his funeral expenses.

The First Baptist Church is at the center of this El Paso view looking northwest. The church was constructed in 1884, on Magoffin Street and San Antonio Avenue, with George W. Baines serving as pastor. By 1896, El Paso had sixteen churches, and Reverend Millican was the pastor at the First Baptist Church.

An 1882 view of San Antonio Avenue and El Paso Street. Heavily laden wagons, drawn by teams of oxen, transported goods up and down the Camino Real before the railroad came. After the railroad reached El Paso, the freight wagons were used to transport goods to places not served by the rails. The early pioneers also used these wagons to move their families to new places.

The Grand Central Hotel, on North Oregon Street, with San Jacinto Plaza in the foreground. Anson Mills and Josiah Crosby built the Grand Central as a luxury hotel in 1883. It was destroyed by fire in 1892. San Jacinto Plaza was where the corrals of the Juan María Ponce de León ranch formerly stood. Ponce de León had obtained a land grant for 211 acres in 1827, and the area became known as Ponce's Ranch.

This photograph of Pioneer Plaza was taken by Ben Wittick in 1882. On the right is the Central Hotel, fronting South El Paso Street, and to the hotel's left is the Casa Grande Dry Goods Store. A sign for the Pony Saloon, which offered entertainment for the men, is tucked up by the tall pole. On the far left is the Mundy Brothers Market, a meat market and wholesaler, with three longhorns out front. The Mundys owned a stock business that exported sheep, cattle, and horses to Mexico and sold meat and livestock in El Paso.

Lightbody and James Store in the Davis Block, sold clothing, boots, hats, shirts, socks, and merchant tailoring. Robert C. Lightbody was the mayor of El Paso from 1885 until 1889 and the leader of the McGinty Club Plug Hat Brigade. The store would later become R. C. Lightbody Clothing Company.

This is an early El Paso City Hall, Fire Department, and Police Department, on the southwest corner of Overland Avenue and Santa Fe Street. When the building was erected, in 1882, a volunteer fire department was organized.

Public education started in El Paso in 1883. This is the Franklin School, at Leon Street and Overland Avenue. Also on Overland Avenue, the Butterfield Overland Mail Company operated a stage stop, and its El Paso building was the largest station on the 2,700-mile-long Overland route. Railroads eventually replaced the stage, and the Butterfield building was torn down.

Occupying themselves at the El Paso County Court House are, from left, Frank Simmons, J. H. Comstock, Judge T. A. Falvey, Captain Jim White, and W. L. Maury. Judge Falvey was a federal district judge who presided over the district of Judge Roy Bean, which included El Paso, Fort Stanton, Del Rio, and other areas. The El Paso County Sheriff's office was moved to the new courthouse in 1886.

The Palace Hotel offered furnished rooms above the Goodman Produce Company, 501 El Paso Street, which sold candy and cigars in addition to produce. The El Paso Vinegar and Extract Company advertised on the side of the building was also owned by S. L. Goodman. Sharing the hotel advertising space, the Southern Pacific reminded passersby "you can keep cool in California," which the people with money would do.

The *El Paso Herald* composing room seen here has a Linotype machine being used by the employees. Invented in 1886 by Otto Mergenthaler, Linotype allowed one man to do the work in composing a newspaper that used to take ten men by hand.

El Paso Street and San Francisco Street had the Mine and Smelter Supply Company on the northwest corner, managed by D. L. Gregg. At this point El Paso was becoming a mining center. In 1887 Robert Towne built a smelter west of downtown. Mining conventions were held in El Paso, and the Texas State School of Mines and Metallurgy, the forerunner of the University of Texas at El Paso, was approved by the state legislature in 1913.

The *El Paso Herald* Building, with A. H. Richards Jeweler in the downstairs front. In a listing for 1903, A. H. Richards was at 103 El Paso Street. The William Jennings Company office was on the third floor, front. On the right side, Felix Martinez had an office upstairs, and the International Book and Stationery Company was downstairs.

A man relaxes on the porch of the Hotel Orndorff at Mills and Mesa streets. The hotel had a bar, like most hotels. The El Paso Cycle Company, on the left side of the picture, was at 308 Mesa Street and was owned by C. D. Freeman.

Saint Clement's Episcopal Church, on Montana Avenue at Campbell. Judge Gaylord Judd Clarke of the 25th District and his wife Frances moved to the region in 1847. In 1867 they named the original Episcopal church after one of their sons, Clement, who had died as an infant. Joseph W. Tays was the first parson of the church, along with being an early investor in the *El Paso Times* newspaper.

A couple and their dog stand before a bungalow on Campbell Street, which is named for Robert F. Campbell, the mayor of El Paso in 1895-96.

Kansas City Consolidated Smelting and Refining Company built a lead and copper smelter in 1887. Most of the employees were from Chihuahua and lived in houses along the Rio Grande in a community that became known as Smeltertown. They named their church San Rosalia, after a town many of the employees were from. In the 1970s, Smeltertown residents had to move because of lead poisoning, and most of the buildings were torn down.

F. C. Cole and H. P. Noake had a carriage and wagon business at the corner of Overland Avenue and Santa Fe Street. Racine Baggage is advertised on the left side of the picture. H. P. Noake manufactured vehicles and harnesses. In Chihuahua, he operated as Noake and DeSmith.

This picture of the McGinty Club Light Guards with their cannon was taken in 1896. The McGinty Club marched in all the El Paso parades and attended every ceremony. In the front row are club members Frank Hughes, Billy O'Brien, Herb Stevenson, Harry Kneeland, Kinney Feathers, and Harry Moss. Standing in the back, from left, are Frederick "Peg" Grandover, Frank G. Gaskey, Henry Ong, Billy Shunman, Captain James J. Longwell, Henry Moore, Thomas Booth, and Jimmy J. Watts.

A Tudor-style house, built in 1892. The First Baptist Church, at 805 Montana Avenue, now owns the house.

Many people pushed for public schools and made education a priority during the early days of El Paso. In this picture, the students are weaving and making baskets. The date May 1884 is written on the chalkboard. By 1896, El Paso had three private schools and five public ones.

This office full of well-dressed men is probably in the El Paso County Courthouse, which is said to have been the main social and business center for town.

Lone Star Horse Shoeing Shop, with the farrier in the middle of the picture, holding the horse's hoof. Tom Newman is second from right.

Texas Rangers on the steps of the El Paso County Courthouse in 1896.
The Texas Rangers battled with robbers and cattle rustlers, and dealt
with problems along the border.

Men gamble at roulette while a waiter brings them beer. A calendar behind them says "Shasta" and "July," and judging by the flags and decorations, the scene may be a 4th of July celebration. Gambling was legal throughout the West at this time.

THE BOOM YEARS

(1900–1909)

Calling itself the Gate City, turn-of-the-century El Paso was the commercial center of the Southwest, served by a host of railroad lines: the Southern Pacific; Texas and Pacific; Atchison, Topeka and Santa Fe; Mexican Central; Rio Grande, Sierra Madre, and Pacific; El Paso–Rock Island; El Paso and Southwestern; and the Galveston, Harrisburg, and San Antonio. The mining industry was going strong, and the custom smelter in El Paso was the world's biggest, employing in the vicinity of 1,200 people.

Twenty miles long, the streetcar line crossed the border and would become electric during the century's first decade. There were many hotels and more being built, and three national banks and a savings bank. Agriculture was becoming a large business, as was ranching and livestock. People were coming to El Paso to invest in the area north of the border and in Mexico.

In 1902, Gustavus Trost moved to El Paso and started an architecture firm in the Guaranty Trust Building. In 1903, he was joined by one of his brothers, Henry C. Trost, and they set up the firm of Trost and Trost, with nephew George Trost helping as a draftsman. Henry Trost was the chief designer. Everett Bradt started with the company, as a clerk, in 1906. In 1908, brother Adolphus Trost joined as a structural engineer. The firm designed more than 300 buildings in El Paso, plus many in New Mexico, Arizona, Colorado, and Mexico. Henry C. Trost was influenced by architects Louis Sullivan and Frank Lloyd Wright. His building styles included Spanish mission, Pueblo, and any other style his clients wanted. Trost designed the first reinforced-concrete buildings in El Paso and New Mexico.

Charles Eddy organized the Alamogordo and Sacramento Railroad to make runs to Cloudcroft, New Mexico, to get timber; but people also rode the Alamogordo and Sacramento Mountain Excursion Train to get away from the summer heat. Many people in El Paso owned cabins in Cloudcroft, and families would spend summers there. Horseback riding was popular in Cloudcroft, and cars weren't very common there until an improved road was built in 1920.

City National Bank is on the left side of El Paso Street, the Eastern Grill is near the streetlight, and the Grand Hotel is across on the right at San Francisco and El Paso. August Andreas was the president and one of the founders of the City National Bank, which was organized in October 1904.

This is the Bailey School, which was built in 1880 and was the oldest public school in El Paso at the time it was closed and torn down in 1945. The Baileys were a prominent family, and one of them was a United States Customs Agent.

Number 1508, a Rock Island Line transcontinental passenger train, crosses the bridge. The Rock Island and the Southern Pacific jointly operated the Golden State Limited passenger service, starting in 1902. El Paso was connected to the rest of the country and Mexico by many train routes. The city is on the route with the least elevation as it traverses the United States between the East and West coasts.

Otis Aultman, the photographer of many pictures in this book, is seated on the right while playing cards. Though titles aren't visible, the reading material under the table includes *Top-Notch Magazine, The Spell of the Yukon* by Robert Service, and the *American Annual of Photography*. Aultman started a club called the Adventurers Club, shortened to the Ad Club, that was an informal group of newsmen, soldiers of fortune, and military men who were in El Paso during the Mexican Revolution and who would get together whenever a few members were in town.

Flooding has long been a problem for the El Paso region and has caused many relocations over the years. La Purisima Socorro Mission, built in 1691, was damaged by floods in 1740 and 1829. Fort Bliss was moved to Concordia in 1868 due to flooding. In 1897, a flood ruined many buildings in El Paso and Juárez. In 2006, the flood control reservoirs overflowed with rain, and there was flooding across the city.

The St. Charles Hotel, upstairs at 301 South El Paso Street, in 1905. The St. Charles Hotel was open until 1996. McBean and Simmons Undertakers is on the left side of the picture, at 305 South El Paso Street, and in the middle of the picture is the Shelton-Payne Arms Company. On the far right side, the El Paso Cornice Works is at 106 West Overland Avenue.

Avenida 16 de Septiembre, with the Ciudad Juárez Customs House on the right. The El Paso Street Railway Company started in 1882, with mules pulling the streetcars. In 1902 the streetcars switched to electric, and Mandy the mule was given a ride on a flatcar to celebrate her retirement. The electric streetcars connected El Paso, Juárez, and Fort Bliss.

As more families moved to El Paso, there were movements to clean up the town, which still had Wild West elements. Among the local organizations, the Woman's Club of El Paso was organized in 1894 and worked tirelessly to improve the city, while a local chapter of the Women's Christian Temperance Union was organized in 1896.

Union Depot opened at 700 San Francisco Street on March 1, 1906, only a year before this picture was taken. Daniel Burnham, the architect, designed the depot to replace the seven different stations used by various railroads. The red-brick, neoclassical building has been restored and is now on the National Register of Historic Places. Pancho Villa is said to have used the tower of the depot as a lookout during the Mexican Revolution.

Agencias de Cambio and Blumenthal Clothier was owned by Bernard and Adolph Blumenthal at 117 South El Paso Street. It was established in 1892. Two of the men in the picture—probably the two on the left—are Bernard Blumenthal and Park W. Pittman. They changed currency and sold clothes.

With old wooden bridge pilings in the foreground, people can be seen on the riverbanks below as a trolley crosses the Santa Fe Street International Bridge.

L. D. Jenkins Curios and Cigars, on Avenida 16 de Septiembre, in Juárez. Jenkins sold photos, postal cards, curios, cigars, canes, drawings, shoes, cut coins, jewelry, and old relics. Our Lady of Guadalupe Church can be seen in the background.

A cattle ranch picnic, with a chuck wagon, plenty of food, cowboys with tin plates and cups, and well-dressed ladies and gentlemen. Ranching and agriculture were the region's main businesses after 1827, when Juan María Ponce de León built his ranch. In 1849, Ponce de León sold the ranch to Benjamin Franklin Coons. Coons built a general store, and the settlement became known as Franklin.

The El Paso Federal Building, on the left, housed the Customs House, the United States Post Office, and the Federal Courthouse. Hotel Sheldon, in the center, was managed by Burt Orndorff. The Grand Central Hotel is on the right, and San Jacinto Plaza in the foreground, with people enjoying a rest on the benches. Fisher Satterthwaite designed the park. He constructed the fence and gazebo, planted elm trees, and created a pond in which alligators were kept.

Cloudcroft Lodge was built in 1901 to accommodate mountain vacationers, some of whom are perhaps at a dance here to celebrate summer. In 1909 the lodge was destroyed by fire.

Among this festive group, some dressed in women's clothing, hatbands have the words "Commercial Travelers, October 7, 1904, Albuquerque." Like Albuquerque, El Paso had a Commercial Club for promoting business. Many such clubs held conventions in El Paso, which had ready access to gambling after most cities in the United States made gambling illegal.

Mining was a major industry in El Paso and provided work of all sorts. This machine shop has a large metal lathe, seen on the right.

Potter and White Drug Store, 4 Plaza Block, with egg drinks for 15 cents and nut-and-fruit sundaes for the same price. Egg drinks were mixed with milk or malted milk and were served at soda fountains in the days before ice cream shakes. In 1903, El Paso had twelve drugstores.

An early Ford vehicle modified for operating on mine rails. El Paso was a big mining center, with silver, copper, and zinc coming into the United States from mines in Mexico, and coal being exported to Mexico. About 3,000 people worked in the custom smelter in El Paso. People and companies involved in the mining industry would come into town to buy supplies, equipment, and materials.

This 1907 photograph was probably taken by William Henry Jackson and is a shot of the Fred Harvey Curio and News Stand at the Union Depot. The Fred Harvey Company partnered with the Santa Fe Railroad and had restaurants and hotels all through the West. Fred Harvey commissioned Native Americans to make high-quality arts and crafts for his stores.

A crowd waits at the Cloudcroft Train Station for passage back to El Paso. The El Paso Woman's Club, Dr. Herbert Stevenson, Joshua Raynolds, the Little Theater Group, and many others helped raise funds to open the Baby Sanitarium in Cloudcroft. Many children in El Paso became sick from heat-related problems in the summers and were sent to the Cloudcroft Baby Sanitarium for its fresh air and for the benefit of their health in general.

This group of men and women in formal clothing may have gathered for a Quinceañera, the celebration of a girl's fifteenth birthday, when she becomes a woman. This rite of passage is still celebrated today and can be a party at home or a more extravagant production.

Aduana Fronteriza, the Ciudad Juárez Customs House, built during the years 1885 to 1889. This Victorian building was where all the merchandise crossing the border was taxed. Railroads carried goods back and forth between the United States and Mexico, but the tracks seen here were for the trolley line that ran between the two countries.

Bryan Bros. Clothing, on the left, was at 320 San Antonio Avenue, with the Palace Theatre beside it. Husselman and Jenkins sold cigars and had pool tables at 322 San Antonio. Elsewhere on the street, the Caples Hotel was run by Mrs. J. F. Crews, while the Silver King Restaurant and Bar had Carl Kirchner as the proprietor. Seen here on the right is the Fred J. Feldman Company, which sold photographic and engineers supplies at 308 San Antonio after moving from 111 El Paso Street.

When people visited El Paso for important events, they came on the train and dressed up for the journey. Travelers from all over the United States and Mexico came to El Paso and Juárez in 1909 to greet the two countries' presidents and witness their historic meeting.

First Baptist Church, at 801 Magoffin Avenue. The street is named after Joseph Magoffin, who built the Magoffin Homestead in 1875 and was elected mayor in 1881. Many nice residences were built in the Magoffin Addition in the 1880s.

The Security Trust and Savings Bank, on Mills Street. Next door is the George D. Kendall Optical Company, with Yale Painless Dentists upstairs. A pure gold crown cost five dollars!

St. Joseph's Hospital, or St. Joseph's Sanatorium, was at 190 Grandview Avenue. Lured by the abundant sunshine, many people moved to the Southwest to cure tuberculosis and other lung problems. El Paso promotions at the time said the city spent $200,000 a year for health conservation and sanitation.

President William Taft was in El Paso on October 16, 1909, to meet with President Porfirio Díaz of Mexico. A presidential breakfast was held for Taft at the St. Regis Hotel, on Oregon Street. Afterward, the president went to the Chamber of Commerce.

On October 16, 1909, the El Paso Federal Building, at the corner of Mills and Oregon streets, was decorated and ready for the historic meeting between presidents William Taft and Porfirio Díaz. The low-flung building behind the poles is the Elite Manufacturing and Confectioners; Pancho Villa held meetings there, and it was his favorite place for a strawberry soda.

El Paso went all-out on the occasion of the Taft-Díaz meeting, with townsmen donning silk top hats and Prince Albert coats. The two presidents met at the center of the International Bridge and were taken in carriages through El Paso with the United States Army Cavalrymen and the Mexican Army as escorts.

El Paso advertised itself as the Gate City, the commercial center of the Southwest. The chief business interests were the mining and smelting of gold, silver, lead, and copper ores. The El Paso Smelting Works employed 1,200 people at this time.

In the afternoon of October 16, 1909, Presidents Taft and Díaz met in Ciudad Juárez. On the right side of this picture is the Juárez Customs House, at Avenida Juárez and Avenida 16 de Septiembre. The Victorian building was restored in 1990 for the Juárez Museum of History.

The United States Delegation
is in the reviewing stand for the
Taft-Díaz meeting, October 16,
1909.

The Juárez Customs House the night of the Taft-Díaz meeting, October 16, 1909. The building was decorated as a Versailles salon with red curtains, pictures of George Washington and Miguel Hidalgo, fine linen, gold and silver Maximilian silverware, and cut crystal. Felix Martinez, of El Paso, gave the presidents gold goblets from his city.

Elks Club, El Paso Lodge 187, Benevolent and Protective Order of Elks. Formerly El Paso's first school building, the Central School, it stood on the corner of Myrtle Avenue and Campbell Street and was built by Bernard and Benjamin Schuster. The building was torn down, and a new Elks Club was built at the same location.

The adobe Mission of Our Lady of Guadalupe (Mission Nuestra Señora de Guadalupe) was inaugurated on January 5, 1662. It was an important stop on El Camino Real de Tierra Adentro, the Royal Road to the Interior. During the 1680 Pueblo Revolt in New Mexico, refugees went south and sought shelter at the mission. The church still stands and has been restored, using the original sketches.

THE MEXICAN REVOLUTION AND WORLD WAR I

(1910–1919)

Fort Bliss was the largest cavalry post in the United States in 1910. The National Guard stationed about 50,000 men at Fort Bliss and other camps in the area during the Mexican Revolution. The troops converted to mechanized units during this time period. Armored cars, long-range artillery, and airplanes started to replace horses and wagons. Many soldiers were brought to the area to guard the border, participate in the Punitive Expedition in pursuit of Francisco "Pancho" Villa, and train for World War I. The war brought more prosperity to El Paso, the supply center for all the military camps.

The many railroads serving El Paso made it the major distribution center for the Southwest. The area's farmland and ranches were advertised as the best in the world. More roads were built, and automobiles became more common. The Texas State School of Mines and Metallurgy was started. Elephant Butte Dam opened in 1916, providing recreation areas and helping with agriculture and flood control.

Many refugees moved to El Paso during the Mexican Revolution. Old Chihuahua families with wealth came to escape the violence. The Mormons, too, fled Mexico. During this time, revolutionaries moved in and out of El Paso. Francisco Madero stayed at the Sheldon Hotel and was entertained by the city's leaders. Pascual Orozco, Abraham Gonzalez, and Pancho Villa led the revolutionary army, and they stayed in town often. Gonzalez established a revolutionary junta on the fifth floor of the Caples Building. Guns and ammunition were purchased in El Paso or passed through the city to be smuggled into Mexico. Uniforms were purchased for the revolutionaries. The Battle of Juárez was fought with the people of El Paso watching from across the river.

Newsmen and photographers arrived from all over to report on the action. Otis Aultman was among them. In March 1912 he took battle pictures of the Orozco Rebellion at Rellano, Chihuahua. Aultman worked for the International News Service and Pathe News. With Bud Fisher, he went to Villa's headquarters to film the Villa-Obregon armies in 1914. That same year, Aultman and Robert Dorman formed a partnership. After Villa's raid on Columbus, New Mexico, on March 9, 1916, Aultman was the first photographer on the scene. He took pictures of the United States Cavalry pursuit, known as the Punitive Expedition. The military action was led by General John J. Pershing; one of his lieutenants was George Patton.

The box canyon near Ojo Caliente is an archaeological site that spans 900 years. The area was occupied by the ancient Anasazi and Mogollon cultures and later was home to Chief Victorio of the Mimbres band, the Warm Springs Apaches. The area was called La Canada Alamosa, then was changed to Monticello Canyon in 1881. The small creek is Alamosa Creek. To the right of the wagon, photographer Otis Aultman can be seen setting up his camera.

The September 16, 1910, inauguration of the Monumento a Benito Juárez (Benito Juárez Monument) in Ciudad Juárez, Mexico, celebrated a century of independence from Spain. Governor Enrique Creel of Chihuahua commissioned Italian sculptors Fransisci Rigalt and Augusto Volpi to oversee the marble project. The monument's four plaques represent the life of Benito Juárez. Mexico declared independence from Spain on September 16, 1810.

An early automobile carries a pair of newsmen up a hill. Newsmen from all over the United States followed the troops during the Mexican Revolution.

Charles Hamilton, known as the Birdman, learned to fly from Glenn Curtiss. In 1910 he did exhibition flights in Tucson and Douglass, Arizona, then came to El Paso and was photographed here at Washington Park. The park is an enjoyable place where many events are still held.

Seeing a Curtiss Pusher in flight in 1910 was very exciting. Exhibition flights such as this one by Charles Hamilton at Washington Park created a lot of interest in airplanes. In 1911, the *El Paso Times* contracted with Hamilton to return and fly over Juárez to look for troop concentrations. He flew over Mexico for twenty-two miles and called himself a flying war correspondent. The United States military was also becoming interested in using airplanes and was involved in research and tests.

El Paso, like most cities in the Southwest, advertised itself as a health center and always needed nurses. This group is the Providence School of Nursing class of 1912.

This fire-gutted shell of a three-story building was a reminder of the dangers of fire in El Paso's dry climate. The sign near the building says "American National Bank will be open for business." In 1905, the Myar Opera House caught fire and the whole block was destroyed. One of the reasons the architect Henry C. Trost was in demand was his use of concrete, which is fire resistant. The odd-looking sphere at upper-right is the globe of a streetlamp.

Tickets to see *Trey O'Hearts* at the Unique Theatre cost 10 cents for adults and 5 cents for children. Released in 1914 by the Universal Film Manufacturing Company, *Trey O'Hearts* was a 15-episode serial based on a novel by Louis Joseph Vance.

The Crystal Theater, in the 100 block of East San Antonio Avenue, flanked by Michelson's Pool and Cigars and Ward's Pharmacy on the right side of the picture. W. T. Hixson Jewelers is on the far right, at 111 San Antonio Avenue.

Providence Hospital opened in 1902 at Upson Avenue and North Santa Fe Street. The horse-drawn ambulance of the firm McBean, Simmons, and Carr is seen here in front of the old Providence Hospital in 1910, with Mr. McBean holding the reins. The hospital advertised its beneficial location in the fresh air away from the noise of the city. The Providence staff was supervised by Miss M. R. Shaver.

The El Paso Chamber of Commerce, front row: Jim Watts, unidentified, George Squires, Jack Keevil, Dan W. Reckhart, William McCoy, Doc Dengler, unidentified; second row: George Ogden, C. E. Kelly, Louis Behr, Anton Van Mourick, Crawford Harvie, W. T. Hixson, Will R. Brown, Frank Behr, two unidentified.

At the construction site for the White House Department Store and Hotel McCoy, at 127 Pioneer Plaza, the construction crew pose near their wooden forms for pouring concrete. Behind them are signs for Tuttle Paint and Glass, on North Stanton Street; Scott White and Company Drugs, on Mills Street; and W. T. Hixson Company Jewelry, at Mesa and Mills. The store building is now the Centre, at 123 Pioneer Plaza, and is on the National Register of Historic Places.

Seen here in 1911, the Posener Building, also known as Little Caples Building, was designed by architect Henry C. Trost and housed the Max Posener Millinery business at Mesa and San Antonio Avenue. The Posener Building was demolished in 1941.

Automotive shop workers assemble an early car—the wheels have wooden spokes.

The *El Paso Herald* Building stands on the left, with the office of Felix Martinez Investments upstairs, in this street scene from about 1912. Emblazoned above the clock is the name A. D. Foster Co., a jewelry firm in the *Herald* Building. Henry C. Trost was the architect of the terra-cotta building in the middle, at 109 Pioneer Plaza, which has the White House Department Store downstairs and the Hotel McCoy, owned by W. M. McCoy, upstairs. The tall building on the right, the Mills Building, was designed by Trost for Anson Mills in 1911.

The El Paso City Hall was in this building at East San Antonio Avenue and Kansas Street from 1899 to 1959. The building cost $57,000 to erect. The signs behind it advertise bicycles and coal. In addition to city business, the City Hall was used for social occasions and functions.

This picture was taken when President Theodore Roosevelt came to El Paso, in March of 1911. Colonel Edgar Z. Steever, Commander at Fort Bliss, is in the carriage.

A celebration in Cloudcroft, New Mexico, in 1911. The Alamogordo and Sacramento Railroad would take people from El Paso up into the mountains for a summer getaway. El Paso residents still go to Cloudcroft in the summer to cool off and enjoy the clean mountain air.

On Mills Street, the Sullivan Machinery Company sold mining machinery. The James A. Dick Company Wholesale Grocers offered a wide variety of products.

Construction began on the Elephant Butte Dam at this site in 1910. The dam allowed El Paso to have a steady supply of water. Many railroad cars' worth of supplies, and the work of many people, were needed to complete the multi-year project.

President Theodore Roosevelt stopped in El Paso while on his way to Arizona for the dedication of the Roosevelt Dam, in March 1911. A United States Army officer is standing behind him.

The Francisco Madero family, being entertained at the home of Mr. and Mrs. Frank Wells Brown, in May of 1911. Madero, one of the leaders of the Mexican Revolution, wanted democracy in Mexico. The rebel armies were in Juárez, trying to set up a provisional government, and Madero used the Sheldon Hotel in El Paso as his headquarters. Many in El Paso supported Madero, and the arms his forces used were bought in town and taken across the Rio Grande,

Over 300 people from El Paso were on hand this day in 1916 for the dedication ceremony for the Elephant Butte Dam, which gave a steady, reliable water supply to El Paso and helped control flooding.

It cost a nickel to see the Universal silent film being shown at this theater. The musicians and conductor here would provide the music accompaniment. El Paso has a very rich musical tradition that is a blend of cultures.

The 1911 Arizona–New Mexico Statehood Jubilee parade anticipated the admission of New Mexico, the forty-seventh state, to the union on January 6, 1912, and of Arizona, the forty-eighth state, on February 4, 1912. The awning of Miller Company Good Cigars can be seen behind the parade crowd.

Looking toward the Franklin Mountains, this view is across San Jacinto Plaza, named in honor of the famous Texas battle of San Jacinto. Chinese elms were planted in the park, behind which, on the left, El Paso Trunk can be seen. Hotel Angelus and Hotel Delmar are in front of the mountain.

In this 1910 photo of a Juárez restaurant, the cooking takes place at a spot in the middle of the tables. Zona Pronaf Mercado, a Juárez public market, had stalls for small businesses. It was torn down in the 1990s, and Plaza de las Americas replaced it. El Mercado Juárez provides the old market experience and is run by the Juárez Municipal Government.

In this image from Fort Bliss, a group of English officers, a doughboy (center), and a medic pose with a pair of water-cooled machine guns and a bulldog carrying a first-aid pack.

The Toltec Building, designed in a Renaissance Beaux-Arts style by Henry C. Trost, is at 602 Magoffin Avenue. Trost was a member of the Toltec Club, which was a men's club inside the building. The Toltec Club was the site of a victory banquet put on by city leaders for Francisco Madero in 1911, during the Mexican Revolution.

Juárez Racetrack always attracted a crowd, with horse races and dog racing featured. Otis Aultman was the official photographer for the track for several years. He took photos of many of the horses and the ends of all the races.

The McGinty Club's muzzle-loading cannon, called the Blue Whistler, was returned to El Paso over the bridge from Mexico in 1911. The Mexican revolutionary armies used the cannon against the Mexican federal troops.

The Longwell Transfer Company, operated by J. J. Longwell at 116-18 San Francisco Street, owned this multipurpose truck. The Remington Typewriter Company was at 204 Texas Avenue, and in 1916 the Draughon's Business College was listed as in the Trust Building. Behind the pole one can just make out the Jenkins Piano Company.

Blumenthals Clothing can be seen at the end of San Antonio Avenue, at 100 South El Paso Street, and in the upper right, the Mills Building, at 303 North Oregon Street. The Mills Building was owned by Anson Mills and was completed in 1911. Henry C. Trost designed the all-concrete structure, and the firm of Trost and Trost had its offices there.

The Texas and Pacific Railroad, run by Jay Gould, raced the Southern Pacific Railroad to bring the first train into El Paso. The Southern Pacific won the race. The Texas and Pacific Railroad Freight Station, seen here in 1912, is now the GLBT Community Center, at 216 South Ochoa Street.

Central Fire Station, 600 East Overland Avenue, in 1915. The El Paso Hose Company No. 1 started out on August 22, 1882, as a volunteer fire department. The company contracted with Sylvester Watts to build a waterworks for the city residents and to provide 25 fire hydrants. When a fire broke out the same year, two buildings were lost because the fire hydrant was across the street, and they only had 100 feet of hose. In 1909, the city went to a paid fire department crew, with W. W. Armstrong as the first fire chief.

This day was the "last time" one could see the 1911 silent movie *From the Bottom of the Sea* at the Alhambra Theater. Starring Mary Pickford and Charles Arling, it was promoted as the "greatest marine picture ever shown."

Coal heating supplies were brought to El Paso by railroad, and the Dawson Fuel Sales Company would load them onto the company truck for delivery to customers, as in this 1913 photo. The Dawson firm was managed by G. M. Hanson at 710 Mills Building. By 1916 there were seven additional wholesale coal suppliers in El Paso.

This Spanish colonial, Moorish-style building, designed by Henry C. Trost, opened in 1914. The Alhambra Theater, at 209 South El Paso Street, had a large organ to provide music for silent movies and live theater. Alhambra Jewelry was at 211 South El Paso, and the Singer Sewing Machine Company was on the right, at 205. The Alhambra became the Palace Theater and is on the National Register of Historic Places.

Streetlights blaze on San Antonio Avenue, with Michelson's Pool and Cigars on the left, and behind it a new building under construction. Across the street is Blumenthal's Clothing, at 300 San Antonio, and on the right is A. J. Fullan Pawnbroker, Diamond Merchant, and Money Lenders, at 102.

In the distance beyond Foutz and Moore Furniture Company, owned by Charles Foutz at 113 North Stanton Street, a towering sign urges locals to "use electric light." In the 1880s, Mayor Joseph Magoffin and the city council organized Brush Electric Company; in 1890 Zach White took it over. Mr. White had electrical generating equipment installed at a plant at Chihuahua Street and Third. In 1889, the state issued a charter to the International Light and Power Company to provide power for El Paso and Juárez.

Live alligators were kept in the fountain pool at San Jacinto Plaza beginning around 1890. The artist Luis Jimenez grew up in El Paso, and his father, a neon sign artist, often took young Luis to see the alligators. As an adult, Luis Jimenez was commissioned to create a sculpture of airbrushed fiberglass, in vibrant colors, for the park. The sculpture, Plaza de los Lagartos, can be enjoyed by all who visit there.

El Paso Rubber Company sold tires from Goodrich (founded in Ohio in 1870) and accessories at 313 San Francisco Street. Drivers would carry their own pumps and patch-kits to fix flats on the road. El Paso Foundry and Machine Company, at 311 San Francisco, was established in 1888 to manufacture iron castings.

Advertising "This Car to Old Mexico," a tour bus run by the Hotel, Taxicab, and Baggage Company took people to see the sites of El Paso and Juárez. One could ride the bus, see some local scenery, and learn some history, much as one can still do by tour bus today.

Even this early in El Paso, many people owned cars, but if they didn't, El Paso Electric Railway Company would bring them downtown, where they could shop, stop at the Coney Island, go to the theater, send a telegram, or catch a train. The Coney Island, on Oregon Street, started as a saloon and gambling house. If someone needed a tailor, U. S. DeVore Tailoring could help. Kelly and Pollard Drugs was established in 1893 by Charles Edgar Kelly, the mayor of El Paso from 1910 to 1915.

This loaded-down vehicle is parked in front of the Southern Motor Company, which according to the 1916 El Paso city directory was at 355 Myrtle Avenue, with M. J. Roseboro as the manager. Republic Trucks were built until about 1929.

This court scene dates from proceedings surrounding the 1915 detention of General Victoriano Huerta, the deposed president of Mexico, who was arrested in the United States for violating neutrality laws. Jailed in El Paso, he was moved to Fort Bliss when El Paso mayor Tom Lea became worried about the crowds at the federal building.

With El Oasis Café and Cran Barata as the backdrop, this street scene is from the Mexican Revolution.

The arrest and imprisonment of General Huerta attracted large crowds and kept El Paso busy. The whole continent was intrigued and awaited news from the city. El Paso had been the center of national attention since the Mexican Revolution started in 1910 and was overflowing with activity, much of it covert. Many people from Mexico moved to El Paso to get away from the war.

During the Battle of Ciudad Juárez, in 1911, the people of El Paso watched the fighting go on for three days, some of them viewing from boxcars and rooftops. Photographer Otis Aultman was often in the middle of the Mexican Revolution battles with his camera.

Baseball has always been popular in El Paso, as can be seen in this photo of Everybody's Baseball Team, which had a soldier on the squad. Everybody's Department Store, managed by I. M. Mayer at Stanton and Texas Avenue, sponsored the team.

City directories list F. G. Billings Company Music Store at 1429 East Boulevard, then at 103 South El Paso Street, while signage on the delivery truck suggests a third address on North Stanton Street. In addition to pianos and other musical instruments, Billings sold Victrolas.

Businesses such as Bixler & Starks Auto Repair Shop heralded the increasing impact of the automobile on life in El Paso, as elsewhere.

With the Hotel Lenox upstairs, the Globe Department Store, run by the Laskin brothers, sold clothing at the corner of East Overland and South Mesa avenues.

The grocery store proprietor at 402 San Francisco Street kept a well-stocked store. His customers who smoked could find Prince Albert and Stag tobacco, cigars, and Nebo cigarettes advertised as "gloriously good." He also sold Imperial Oats, pineapples, apricots, melons, bananas, and even locks and brooms.

The El Paso Police Department was established in 1884. Here, in front of Liberty Hall, on Overland Avenue, two motorcycle officers examine one of the tires on their Harley-Davidsons, perhaps with a mind to replace it with a new Firestone. Christmas greetings can be seen in the windows. Across the street is the Elliott-Garrett Auto Company. F. J. Garrett was the manager.

The owner of this parade-ready company truck, El Paso Dairy Company operated at a succession of addresses. These included 423 North Oregon Street, in 1916, with A. G. Foster as general manager, and 423 Mesa Avenue, in 1922, with J. A. Smith as manager and secretary. Price Dairy bought the firm in 1927, and a little later it became Price's Creameries.

The Bijou Theatre, at 202 South El Paso Street, is showing *The Leap from the Water Tower*, an episode of a serial with Helen Holmes, produced by J. D. McGowan. The Bijou has nice stained-glass windows. Built in 1906, it started out as the Standard Theatre. A clothier on the right is having a January sale. On the left is the Hotel National, at 210 ½ South El Paso Street, run by M. S. Medlock.

Behind the bar and between the moose heads mounted at the Gem Saloon, one of several signs proclaims the establishment of a union bar, and another advertises Pschorr-Brau Munchen Flaschen Bier. In 1888, the Gem Saloon and Gambling was at 127 South El Paso Street, with J. J. Taylor and George Look in charge. In the early days, the Gem had a vaudeville theater, too. Gambling became illegal in El Paso in 1905.

Traffic at the intersection of Mills and Mesa is controlled by an El Paso police officer using a hand-operated traffic signal. Looking east on Mills Street, this view includes the Commercial National Bank on the corner; C. B. Hudspeth was bank president. Farther down the block at 206 Mills Street is the Success Café, whose proprietor was Mrs. R. C. Woods.

A group portrait of the El Paso baseball team. In 1884, El Paso organized a baseball team, called the El Paso Blues because they wore blue uniforms. By 1886, the El Paso Browns, with brown uniforms, were the pride of the city, and merchants closed their stores on Saturday so everyone could go to their games. The McGinty Club Band played music at the games, and fellow member Charles J. Jones managed the team.

An early race car, license plate number El Paso 6900, has pulled up in front of the Ramming Motor Company, a Buick and Mercer dealer. On the right is the Acme Modern Laundry Company, at 901 East Missouri Street.

Runa Plays Cupid, starring Runa Hodges, was playing at the Grecian Theater at 219 South El Paso Street. After a movie, Phil Young's Café and Oyster House was a nice place to have dinner and a drink. Upstairs was the Simona Hotel. Given Brothers Shoe Company, at 215 South El Paso Street, is on the right side of the picture.

These men are walking across the bridge at the Elephant Butte Dam during a military inspection. One of them is Captain Lewis T. Morey of the United States Army, Fort Bliss. The dedication ceremony for the dam was held in 1916. At the time, Elephant Butte Lake was the largest man-made lake in the United States.

Featuring *Dancer and the King* on this date, the Alhambra Theater at 209 South El Paso Street had a plaster facade with an ornate design. The building originally included the two smaller ones on either side of it. The Rowen & Walker Saloon and the Singer Sewing Store can be seen on the right. A man is getting his boots shined in front of the theater.

Posing in 1914 with two young donkeys, the Adventurers Club, formed by Otis Aultman, would meet, go on adventures, or just socialize whenever they were in El Paso. At various times, members of the informal club included Tracy Richardson, a soldier of fortune in the Mexican Revolution, and General John Pershing.

The Lone Star Motor Company sold Hupmobiles from the Hupp Motor Company. The make was built in Detroit from 1909 to 1940. Lone Star was listed at 355 Myrtle Avenue in 1915, and at 1500 Texas Avenue in 1936.

Hotel Paso del Norte, at El Paso Street and San Antonio Avenue, opened in 1912 after El Paso businessmen Felix Martinez, Horace Stevens, and Zach White helped raise money to build it. A luxury hotel in the Beaux-Arts style, it had brick walls, with stone and concrete, and Trost and Trost later added a tenth-story ballroom. Seen here while under construction, the hotel still stands, now named the Camino Real, with an added seventeen-story tower.

On the corner of San Antonio Avenue and El Paso Street is the First National Bank Building, built in 1883 for Joshua Raynolds, at 109 East San Antonio Avenue. John Wesley Hardin, a notorious gunfighter killed in 1895, is said to have had his law office on the second floor. First National Bank and American National Bank merged in 1914, and in 1915, F. H. Bruns Dentist Office and Pullans Diamond Merchants & Money Lenders operated from the building.

Weston's Perfection Bread Bakery Truck and staff, in 1918. The G. W. Weston Restaurant was at 320 San Antonio Avenue. The hat on the woman says Globe Mills Flour, which was from the El Paso Grain and Milling Company. A little to her right, the William Rosing Clothing Company can be seen, at 320 San Antonio Avenue.

This gathering is at the Cooley residence at Rio Grande and Florence Street. One of the four ladies is Florence Milby.

The University Club, on the top floor of the Martin Building, April 1918. The seven-story Martin Building, at 215 North Stanton Street, was purchased by El Paso Electric Company in 1950.

Operated by El Paso Electric Company, the Camp Grande Sightseeing Coach allowed one to see Juárez. During the Mexican Revolution, in 1911, Francisco Madero attacked the town of Casas Grandes, but the Mexican federal troops defeated his revolutionary army there. Later, General Orozco and General Villa captured Juárez.

United States Cavalry officers from Fort Bliss are on review as a car, license plate El Paso 9191, goes by with dignitaries. On a separate occasion, a ceremony was given for General Pershing and his troops when they returned from the Punitive Expedition. The parade to honor the returning National Guard and Army troops was held in El Paso on February 6, 1917.

The United States Army Infantry marches north on South El Paso Street, passing through Pioneer Plaza. The banner draped crossing the street reads "Texas Headquarters" as a welcome. At the left side of the photo, the Chihuahua Exchange, Casa de Cambio, was managed by Miguel Gutierrez and was in the City National Bank Building. On the far right, people watch the parade from the balconies of the *Herald* building.

The Automobile Years

(1920–1939)

Pancho Villa was shot and killed at Parral on July 20, 1923. Jesus Salas Barraza, a Durango politician, confessed to the killing. He was sentenced to 20 years in prison but was pardoned three months later and set free.

El Paso became a big convention center during the 1920s, due to Prohibition. The Chamber of Commerce advertised El Paso as the "Gateway to Mexico," and Juárez attracted the bars that were now illegal in the United States. El Paso was also selling its climate and advertising itself as a health center. Many of the people living in El Paso had moved there to get away from unhealthy climates in other parts of the United States or to escape the Mexican Revolution. Soldiers stationed at Fort Bliss often stayed in the area after completing their military service.

The automobile allowed growth to spread, and developers sold homes in the Grandview, Sunset Heights, Five Points, Kern Place, and Alta Vista neighborhoods. Skyscrapers appeared downtown. Trucks delivered goods between different areas of El Paso and between cities. El Paso had stockyards and packing plants and three oil refineries. The El Paso Smelter increased in size, and the Nichols Copper company opened a plant. With more than 200 factories by 1930, El Paso was a retail and wholesale center.

The Great Depression affected El Paso somewhat less than it did the rest of the United States but more than it did the rest of the Southwest. Closure of the First National Bank hurt manufacturing and other businesses. In 1932 there were 20,000 people on relief programs locally. Franklin D. Roosevelt's New Deal programs kept people working, starting in 1933, but El Paso lost population, due to the loss of jobs. Architect Henry C. Trost died at the age of 73 in September 1933.

After a gale blew down the old flagpole at Fort Bliss, a dedication ceremony for the new flagpole was held April 15, 1920. Fort Bliss was at Smith's Ranch from 1849 to 1851, Magoffinsville from 1854 to 1868, Concordia from 1868 to 1876, Franklin in 1878 and 1879, and in Hart's Mill from 1879 to 1893. In 1893, Fort Bliss located on the Lanoria Mesa, after El Paso community leaders contributed money to buy the land.

The A. D. Foster Company Jewelers in the *Herald* Building promised its customers "Our Wedding Rings Assure Happy Marriages." In addition to rings, the store sold collector's spoons commemorating the Mexican Revolution, and Gorham silver.

The William G. Walz Company, at 500 San Francisco Street, sold Victor talking machines, phonographs, and records. Victor Talking Machine Company was started by Eldridge Johnson. In 1929, the company was sold, and Radio-Victor became a division of the Radio Corporation of America, or RCA Victor. This store had many styles to choose from, even one player shaped like a piano.

Designed by Henry C. Trost in 1914 and opened in 1916, El Paso High School, at Schuster Avenue and Virginia Street, is the oldest high school in Texas still operating and is on the National Register of Historic Places. It's a classical-revival building with Corinthian columns. The classrooms were designed for natural light and cross ventilation.

This cockfighting scene is at Plaza de Gallos, a ring in Juárez.

Members of the El Maida Shrine in El Paso stand by, horns ready, in this 1923 National Photo Company shot. El Maida, the Temple of the Nobles of the Mystic Shrine, was chartered in 1909.

Children of South El Paso, on South Kansas Street, pose for Otis Aultman in front of an adobe building.

When the first El Paso concrete plant was opened, in 1910, 1250 barrels of the El Toro brand were produced each day. Increasingly, construction warehouses like this one would have abundant supplies of the material.

The showroom for this store suggests it carried a wide variety of merchandise such as the railroads brought to El Paso from all over the continent, but it also sold goods from the local Hoyt Furniture Company, which started at 315 El Paso Street then moved to 109-13 San Francisco Street.

The Red Cap Messenger Service, managed by Lou C. Rea, had a large crew of young El Paso bicyclists ready to deliver. The Red Cap Messenger Service was at 212 ½ Santiago. Many cities still have bicycle messenger services.

The three men posing for Otis Aultman inside an arena are probably fellow members of the Adventurers Club. The city of El Paso made gambling illegal in 1905, so the business moved to Juárez. There were forty gambling businesses in El Paso when it was outlawed, so the city gave up considerable tax and license revenue.

Two baseball players join a group of men and women for porch relaxation after the game. Some of the men are drinking Falstaff beer. Baseball was very popular in the 1920s, so newspapers started to add sport sections, and games were broadcast via the young medium of radio.

This 15-story building, completed in 1930, is the O. T. Bassett Tower, at 301 Texas Avenue. It is art deco, has a brick face with limestone and granite, decorative metalwork, a marble floor in the lobby, and has 10 eagles on the top floor. On the left, street level, is the Rio Grande Paint Store. In the storefronts on the right are Don Thompson's, a barber shop, and a beauty supply store. Next door is the City Club, with the Hotel Herbert upstairs. The Texas Grand Theatre and the Texas Grand Hotel are down the street at 421 Texas Avenue.

Pool halls were social gathering places that were always very popular. During Prohibition, many of the saloons became billiards halls, restaurants, or soda fountains.

As in this school group of well-dressed young women and men, boys at the time wore corduroy or wool knickers with knee-length stockings. Knickers were symbolic of boyhood and usually were worn until the last year of high school.

Many people did not have refrigerators, even though many models were available. Instead, homes had iceboxes, so ice was delivered and sold in blocks by the pound. The J. B. Spears and J. W. Miller Ice Company was at 2300 Texas Avenue in 1922.

The cowgirl and cowboy seen here are part of the long tradition of rodeo in the El Paso area. In 1936, the Cowboys Turtles Association was formed. They became the Rodeo Cowboys Association in 1945 and the Professional Rodeo Cowboys Association in 1975. The El Paso County Coliseum opened in 1942, and the International Livestock Show and Rodeo has been held there ever since then.

The first rodeo in El Paso took place in 1896. In 1902, the Texas Livestock Association Convention came to town, and in 1929, the El Paso Commercial Club, with William Tolbert and J. C. Peyton, sponsored the Ranchman's Reunion and Rodeo. In 1934, the Chamber of Commerce held the Southwestern Livestock Show. When Red Harrington rode Five Minutes to Midnight, it was in front of an enthusiastic crowd.

Clown Pinky Gist, real name Clarence W. Gist, worked with trained mules in his act and performed at many rodeos. His mules were named Freckles, Mickey, and Peanuts. Gist was born in 1892 and died in 1970.

This image is thought to be from the 1936 El Paso Sun Carnival Parade, at the start of the Texas State Centennial celebration. The Tigua Pueblo had marchers in the parade, and the Mescalero Apache had a float. These riders are Apache, wearing squash-blossom necklaces, moccasins, and headbands.

Nuestra Señora de la Concepción del Socorro, Our Lady of the Immaculate Conception of Socorro, nave and alter. Marvin Eickenroht took this picture of the Mission Socorro on May 25, 1936. The elaborately framed carved stations of the cross and vigas can be seen. The Franciscan mission was started after the New Mexico Pueblo Revolt, in 1682. The church has been rebuilt because of floods. The Piro Indians named it Mission Socorro, after the area in New Mexico they were from.

Marvin Eickenroht also shot this photo of the Presidio Chapel of San Elizario, on May 25, 1936. This was a presidio built by Spain. The chapel was built in 1882, but the interior was redone after a fire in 1935. The chapel is part of the San Elizario Historic District, which is set up like a Spanish colonial town.

This wall photographed by Marvin Eickenroht in 1936 is what remained of the Simeon Hart Grist Mill. Simeon Hart married Jesusita Siqueiros of Chihuahua in 1849. They moved to El Paso del Norte and started a flour mill, El Molino, which contracted with the United States military to provide flour. Simeon Hart was an El Paso County judge from 1852 to 1854.

The El Paso Highway Patrol under Captain Allen Falby, with their Harley-Davidson motorcycles. Bill Harley and Arthur Davidson developed their first motorcycle in 1903 and opened their first factory in 1906. In 1907, they started to sell motorcycles to police departments. They were used along the border, during the Mexican Revolution, in the hunt for Pancho Villa. During World War I and World War II, many of the Harley-Davidson motorcycles went to war with the United States military.

Although it is not known what brought these men and the girl together, it looks like they are standing in front of the business where the men work. The ones on the left are proudly wearing campaign hats, so may be veterans. Perhaps they are waiting for a parade.

Super Chevrolet Service and Good Will Used Cars are ready for business in El Paso. William C. Durant started Chevrolet Motor Company in 1911, in Michigan, with race car driver Louis Chevrolet. General Motors bought Chevrolet in 1917. This truck is a 1936 Master Commercial Chevrolet half-ton pickup, and the car is a 1936 Chevrolet two-door sedan.

These Borden's Fine Dairy Products delivery trucks are from Borden's Produce Company, which was at 2215 Myrtle Avenue. Borden's opened its El Paso plant in 1932. Milkmen brought dairy products to the front doorsteps of houses and to businesses. Milk and cream came in glass bottles, which many people now collect.

Photographer Dorothea Lange took this May 1937 photo on the international bridge between Juárez and El Paso. In 1935, Lange married Paul Schuster Taylor, an agricultural economist, and they documented rural poverty and migrant laborers. She was among the Farm Security Administration photographers whose now-famous work was given free to newspapers across the country.

In June 1937, Dorothea Lange photographed these United States Department of Agriculture inspectors checking shoppers' packages as they returned to El Paso from Juárez.

In her work for the Farm Security Administration, Dorothea Lange documented the effects of the Great Depression upon migrant workers. She wanted to motivate people and agencies to see the effects of the Depression and take action to change the situation. In June 1938, she took this photo of a woman waiting in El Paso for a streetcar back to Juárez.

The Multicultural Gateway

(1940–1980)

During World War II, Fort Bliss expanded as an antiaircraft artillery training center. Covering more than a million acres, the Army base became the largest in the United States. In 1941, a $10-million building program was initiated, and the following year, Biggs Field started training B-17 and B-24 bomber crews. After the war, the renamed Biggs Air Force Base became part of the United States Strategic Air Command. By 1950, the Fort Bliss and Biggs Field payroll was $20 million a year. In 1957, the United States Air Defense Center became a major employer in El Paso. Many businesses profited by this growth and provided goods for the bases, and many of the military people retired in El Paso and went on to second careers.

After World War II, large numbers of servicemen took advantage of the G.I. Bill to further their educations. The College of Mines and Metallurgy became Texas Western College, in 1949, and the University of Texas at El Paso, in 1967.

With all this growth, housing and transportation needs had to be met. The federal government offered loan guarantees. The cattle, transportation, and mining industries continued to grow, and the smelter in El Paso was still the largest in the West. Iron ore, copper, and coal arrived from New Mexico to be processed. A metal refinery and three oil refineries, together with foundries, packing plants, two brick plants, and a cement plant, provided many jobs. Electronics companies also moved to the area. Large wholesale houses in El Paso sold goods throughout Mexico and the Southwest, and garment factories produced clothing. Federal and state banking interests facilitated investment, irrigation kept the area fertile for agriculture, and Elephant Butte Dam provided power.

Tourism was still big in the area, and many people stopped in El Paso while on their way to California. The Scenic Drive offered views of Texas, New Mexico, and Mexico. People went back and forth across the border for shopping and other activities. El Paso also served as the main shopping destination for people in southeastern New Mexico. The social programs of the federal government paved roads, built parks and schools, and enhanced the cultural aspects of El Paso.

The Fort Bliss parade fields, with the First United States Cavalry Division group, in March 1941. In front are the Seventh Cavalry regiment, the Eighth Cavalry, Fifth Cavalry, Twelfth Cavalry, Artillery, and mechanized equipment. In the early days of Fort Bliss, the United States Cavalry was stationed there to patrol the border. In 1943, with World War II in progress, the cavalry era was coming to an end, and the men became foot soldiers in the Pacific.

A United States Army parade moves south on Mesa Street on Armistice Day 1941, with a horse unit and the Army band following the motorcycles. In 1919, President Woodrow Wilson established Armistice Day to commemorate the November 11, 1918, signing of the Armistice to end World War I. President Wilson wanted to be sure that we did not forget the tragedies of war. The holiday was changed to Veterans Day in 1954, so that we could honor all veterans.

Crowds overflowed at the Union Depot on September 25, 1948, in anticipation of the arrival of President Harry S. Truman. The president gave a speech about the Democratic Party's interest in issues relating to the West. The federal government had spent more than $20 million on the Rio Grande reclamation project, he noted, which irrigated 160,000 acres in the area. Reclamation projects also provided the West with electricity. President Truman asked the people of El Paso to be sure to vote a straight Democratic ticket.

The four-story Blumenthal Building had the Officers Club on the third floor during World War II. Ellanay Theater opened in 1918. The large building in the background opened in 1912 and had the White House Department Store on the first three floors and the McCoy Hotel on the fourth to seventh floors. The tempting window displays of the White House lured shoppers for decades.

This Sun Bowl football game of January 1, 1946, was played between the University of New Mexico and Denver University. New Mexico won, 34-24, in front of a capacity crowd of 15,000. At the time, the stadium was at Texas Western College, which later became the University of Texas at El Paso. The first Sun Bowl was held in 1935 at the El Paso High School Stadium as a fund-raising event.

On the grandstand at Union Depot, September 25, 1948, President Truman is on the left, then Texas Governor Beauford H. Jester and Mrs. Belle Davis Thomason next to him. Mrs. Thomason's husband, Robert Thomason, was a member of the Texas State House of Representatives, then mayor of El Paso, and the United States representative from Texas in 1931–47. In 1948, he became a judge in the United States District Court for the Western District of Texas.

Viewed from Pioneer Plaza looking east, the 19-story, art deco Hilton Hotel was Conrad Hilton's eighth hotel and his first high-rise. Located at 106 Mills Avenue, it was built by R. E. McKee Company in 1930. Elizabeth Taylor lived in the penthouse when she was married to Nicky Hilton. It became the Plaza Hotel in 1963 when Hilton built a new hotel near the airport. The hotel is on the National Register of Historic Places and is under renovation as of 2008 as part of the downtown revitalization plan.

The first train of the Southern Pacific Railroad entered El Paso on May 13, 1881. Nearly a century later, photographer Bruce Harris captured this view of the Southern Pacific Railroad Bridge.

El Paso International Airport owed its beginnings to a visit by Charles Lindbergh, in 1927. El Paso Aero Club drew up the plans for the airport. On September 8, 1928, the dedication ceremony was held for the Municipal Airport, with Mayor Robert Thomason giving a speech predicting that El Paso would become a future air center. El Paso has always been a transportation center and airplanes were part of the progression.

Built in 1887, but having undergone some changes, the Merrick Building, at 301-03 South El Paso Street, is Queen Anne style with Romanesque details. At the time of this photo, the St. Charles Hotel was upstairs from the Hollywood Cafe. Now an apartment building, with businesses downstairs, the Merrick is on the National Register of Historic Places. Charles Merrick was an official orator in the McGinty Club, a merchant tailor, and the Myar's Opera House manager.

Like the Merrick Building, this one, the Martin Building, is listed on the National Register of Historic Places. Located at North Stanton Street and Mills Avenue, it was the El Paso Electric Company building for 60 years, until 1979.

Scenic Point was created in the 1920s as a lookout in the Franklin Mountains to attract tourists and provide an enjoyable excursion for the people of El Paso. Scenic Drive was paved during the Great Depression. In this picture, a young woman enjoys the view from the rocks above El Paso in the 1940s.

Roberts-Banner Building, on the southwest corner of Mills Avenue and North Mesa Street, was built by Deming cattlemen B. Roberts and W. M. Banner in 1910. The exposed-concrete building was designed by Trost and Trost and is at 215 North Mesa Street.

The Hotel Paso del Norte rooftop ballroom is very elegant and has a wonderful view of the surrounding area. Of all the older hotels in El Paso, the Paso del Norte is the most luxurious. Many businessmen, cattlemen, musicians, government dignitaries, movie stars, and politicians have stayed at the hotel. It has been remodeled in all of its splendor and is now the Camino Real Hotel.

199

Hotel Paso del Norte can be seen at the end of East San Antonio Avenue. To the right of it are American Furniture, Suky Imports, Mayfair, Chico's, and the Guarantee Shoe Company, which sold Florsheim Shoes at 211 East San Antonio Avenue.

Notes on the Photographs

These notes, listed by page number, attempt to include all aspects known of the photographs. Each of the photographs is identified by the page number, photograph's title or description, photographer and collection, archive, and call or box number when applicable. Although every attempt was made to collect all data, in some cases complete data was unavailable due to the age and condition of some of the photographs and records.

HISTORIC PHOTOS OF
EL PASO

El Paso is a city with an international history and culture that is tied to the Rio Grande. Native Americans followed the river and traded with other groups that lived near it. In 1598, Don Juan de Oñate traveled north with a large caravan from Zacatecas, Mexico, to what became known as El Paso del Norte. Near San Elizario, Oñate claimed the area for Spain, and it became a trade center along El Camino Real, the Royal Highway, which went north all the way to the Española Valley in New Mexico.

With the Treaty of Guadalupe Hidalgo, in 1848, the Rio Grande became the international boundary between the United States and Mexico, and El Paso became a town of westernmost Texas. *Historic Photos of El Paso* includes hundreds of images of this great American city, including government, businesses, schools, architecture, military history, and other subjects of historical interest, all showcased in vivid black-and-white.

SANDRA FYE graduated from the University of New Mexico with a bachelor of arts degree in geography and an English minor. She is Registrar at the National Museum of Nuclear Science and History, in Albuquerque. Her favorite place in El Paso is the El Paso Museum of Art. She became interested in the history of El Paso when she saw an Otis Aultman photograph album about the Mexican Revolution. A book about the architect Henry C. Trost added to her interest. She likes photography, history, and art. Fye has written *Historic Photos of Albuquerque,* also available from Turner Publishing Company.

www.ingramcontent.com/pod-product-compliance
Lightning Source LLC
Chambersburg PA
CBHW062004150426

42812CB00013BA/2540